Grief Recovery 101

*How to get back up when blindsided
by the death of someone you love*

Joe McKeever
with Bertha Fagan McKeever

David Russell Tullock

Parson's Book Publishing
Porch. & Company
Turning words into books & Turning books into bread

Grief 101: How to get back up when blindsided by the death of someone you love
ISBN: Softcover 978-1-949888-22-5
Copyright © 2017 by Joe and Bertha McKeever

To order additional copies of this book, contact:

Parson's Porch Books
1-423-475-7308
www.parsonsporch.com

Parson's Porch Books is an imprint of **Parson's Porch & Book Publishers** in Cleveland, Tennessee, which has a double focus. We focus on the needs of creative writers who need a professional publisher to get their work to market, **&** we also focus on the needs of others by sharing our profits with those who struggle in poverty to meet their basic needs of food, clothing, shelter and safety.

Grief Recovery 101

Contents

Dedication

Joe: *To Margaret Ann. Thank you for a thousand gifts over fifty-two-plus years of marriage. You left me better and stronger than how you found me.*

Bertha: *To Gary. You were the perfect embodiment of one who loved his wife as Christ loved the church and gave Himself for her.*

"In the evening, my wife died. And in the morning I did as I was commanded" (Ezekiel 24:18).

"We do not want you to be uninformed, brethren, about those who are asleep, that you may not grieve, as others who have no hope" (I Thessalonians 4:13).

"Everyone has got to die, but I have always believed an exception would be made in my case. Now what?" --William Saroyan, 1908-1981

Introduction

No one plans to become an authority on grief. No kid in the seventh grade announces to the classroom that when he grows up he intends to write books and lead conferences and preach sermons dealing with grief.

Grief happens when we least expect it.

Grief blindsides us. No one is ever quite prepared for the impact of such a blow.

Grief is the emotional response we experience when death takes a loved one. The more they meant to us, the greater the pain.

The only way to escape grief in this life is to exit early. Even then, we leave those we love to deal with their own grief by our departure.

Grief is not par for the course; it is the course.

The textbook calls grief a "multifaceted response to the loss of someone or something that has died, to which a bond or affection was formed."

Grief, we are told, is the tribute of love we pay to the one we have lost. If we did not care, we would not hurt.

A pastor asked me to travel to his church and address a gathering of the widowed on the subject of "living with grief." I knew what he had in mind, but said, "I don't want to live with it. I want to stomp that sucker, to drive a stake through its heart!"

You'd like to get past grief, if possible, and emerge on the other side whole and intact, as quickly as you're able.

I hope we can help. My wife Bertha and I have grieved over the deaths of loved ones, just as everyone else has, I expect. And we have buried our mates, our life-partners, both somewhat unexpectedly. We have been there, experienced that, and had our hearts broken over it. We have shed enough tears for several lifetimes, it feels.

None of what follows is theoretical. It's all practical and down to earth. It's our story.

At a meeting of our denominational leadership in Alexandria, Louisiana, the chairman asked for prayer for E. J. Bradshaw whose wife had died the day before. An hour later, during the break, I bumped into this colleague. "Brad," I said incredulously, "What are you doing here? They said your wife died yesterday."

He answered, "My wife died in the evening and in the morning, I did as I was commanded."

I said, "What? What are you talking about?"

"That's in Ezekiel," he said. "24:18. God told Ezekiel his wife was going to die and he was to go forward with what the Lord had commanded."

A few years later, when my wife died, one of the many phone calls came from Brad. He began the conversation with this: "Joe, 'my wife died in the evening and in the morning I did as I was commanded.'"

I said, "Thank you, my friend. I will try to go forward and do as the Lord leads."

That's what this little book is about, going forward. How do we do that? And what can the hurting do to hurry the process along?

When the pain is new and the grief is fresh, something inside us protests that we don't want to get past it, that to do so would mean forgetting this one so dear to our heart. In her chapter, Bertha tells how the knife piercing her heart after Gary's death was a constant reminder of her love for him. But when her heart began to heal and the knife was no longer there, she feared it meant she was forgetting him, the last thing she wanted.

No one is talking about forgetting.

We're talking about healing. We are talking about learning to get up and get back in the game, learning to function again, to go forward and see what God has for us the next day and the day after that.

A day or two after Margaret died, I wrote in my journal, "People tell me, 'you will see her again,' and 'she's with the Lord.' I know that. I have the eternity thing down pat. It's getting through today that I'm having trouble with."

Now...

Neither of us is a grief counselor or a therapist. I'm a Baptist preacher (with a side helping of blogging and cartooning) and Bertha is a pastor's wife and an English teacher (high school and college all her adult life).

We're both like the person interviewed on television after a tornado has ripped through their town. We can say what we saw and how it felt, but not so much what caused it or what it means or where to go from here.

We're survivors. But more a witness than anything.

We saw grief. Grief tore through our homes and ripped out our hearts and left us in shambles.
Even so...

We hope someone finds something in here to be a catalyst for healing.

One more thing you need to know.

Thirteen months after Margaret died and twenty-one months after Gary died, Bertha Fagan and I met for the first time. Eleven months later, we married.

Bertha Pepper Fagan was married to Dr. Gary Fagan, a preacher of the gospel and a seminary classmate of mine, for over 52 years. Gary and Bertha pastored churches across the country, and then went as missionaries to Malawi and Brazil. In retirement, they moved back home to the Jackson, Mississippi area

14

where Gary began serving Southern Hills Baptist Church. One Sunday in May of 2014, he preached twice, then had an aneurysm that night. He died ten days later.

A year after my wife went to Heaven in January 2015, our son announced he would be moving his family two states away to be closer to his job. I would have no family member nearby, and no reason to remain in metro New Orleans where we had lived since 1990. I began praying for the Lord to send the one whom He would choose as "the love of the rest of my life."

Bertha and I met for lunch on February 15, and within the week knew the Lord had put us together. The rest, as they say, is history.

Part three is Bertha's story. While Joe is writing most of this, Bertha has been involved in the development of the book. Her suggestions have made it better than it would have been otherwise. It is in every way, *their* book.

PART 1

The Grief Arrives

Grief happens when you least expect it and are completely unprepared for it.

How I became so knowledgeable about grief. (I sure didn't volunteer!)

My wife died suddenly.

On a Friday morning in January of 2015, Margaret and I had spent an hour at the breakfast table as we usually did.

After breakfast, she went back to bed. Her physical ailments were always warring against her, the pain was constant, and her energy level was never very high. Even walking into the kitchen was an ordeal for her.

Shortly after finishing my blog, I closed the laptop, took my morning shower and got dressed. Sometime around 10 o'clock, I was lying on the bed in the back bedroom reading a novel when Margaret called down the hall. "I'm going to drive myself to the nail salon and get a pedicure. I'll be back in a little while."

My last word to my wife of 52-plus years was, "Okay!"

Sometime around noon, Ochsner Hospital called. "Sir, you need to come to the emergency room now. We have your mother."

I said, "My wife."

"Sir, we have your wife. You need to come to the emergency room now."

That's all they would say.

We were down to one car, since Margaret had not been driving for a long time. Only recently had she wanted to recapture some measure of independence and was driving a little in the immediate area. I called Julie, our daughter-in-law, to come get me. Our pastor's secretary, Friday was her day off. She was just putting away groceries. "I'll be right there," she said.

When we walked into the hospital, the emergency room doctor met us. "We think your wife had a massive heart attack. And sir, she went over one hour with no heartbeat. We know she's had major brain damage; we don't know how much."

Welcome to real life.

As a pastor for over 53 years, I had walked into thousands of hospital rooms with church members and friends. I must have preached a thousand funerals, including for my parents and Margaret's parents.

But nothing had ever hit me like this.

Nothing prepares you for such news.

The following Wednesday night we signed the papers for them to unplug. Her body had responded to nothing, although the medical team ran a hundred tests and tried all sorts of maneuvers and treatments.

My wife took her last breath Thursday morning, January 29, 2015.

The doctors decided Margaret probably had a pulmonary embolism and not a heart attack. "We'd have to do an autopsy to be sure," they said. We didn't need that. The Lord had taken her and she was with Him.

I would do my best to say with Job, "The Lord giveth; the Lord taketh away; blessed be the name of the Lord."

As I type this, it has been two years and two months. But the pain is still fresh and will never go away. My eyes tear up at the memory of all of this.

When I read the chapter in which Bertha tells of Gary's death, I wept with her.

Components of grief.

What exactly was going on inside me, I wondered. What was causing me to hurt so badly and to feel so sad?

I'm not one given to introspection. But in time, I decided my grief was composed of sadness over Margaret's death, compounded by a lifetime of memories, a good deal of regrets, a touch of anger, and perhaps some fear.

Fully one-half of my grief was *sadness* over missing my wife. I missed her touch, the sound of her voice, and her sharp mind. I missed her involvement in my life.

Margaret was not a writer, but was a great reader, which gave her excellent instincts as to what worked in my writing and what didn't. So, sitting at the breakfast table, she would want me to read my latest blog. Often, she would listen quietly, then interrupt to say, "That's the wrong word," and suggest the one I should have used. We would discuss that, I would make the correction, and continue reading. If she liked the article, she said so. Her approval was better than any editor's acceptance check. But she was just as likely to say, "Well...who do you think is going to be interested in this?" Or even, "That's boring, don't you think?" I smile at the memory. We all need someone who can question what we are doing but who remains on our team, completely committed to us.

In the weeks after she died, I would come out of a church where I'd just preached and start to call her to say how things had gone, since I knew she'd been praying. But I couldn't. And I wept.

In the late 1970s, we had gone to marriage counseling. The culprit--the enemy to every preacher's marriage I ever encountered--was my tendency to put everything and everyone ahead of my family. The stories I could tell, but won't! Suffice it to say, I had some serious adjustments to make in my priorities to save my marriage and to honor my commitments to God, to this good woman, to my family.

After Margaret's death when I began writing about her, people would fill my mailbox with notes saying, "You had an amazing marriage" and "I wish I'd had a marriage like yours." Eventually, I felt the need to share some of the challenges we had faced and problems we had dealt with. To leave the impression that ours was the perfect marriage would only discourage others struggling with the same issues that had plagued us.

Anyone who can look back over half a century of married life without regrets is not being honest, in my opinion. We are all sinners. When we marry, we join ourselves to another breaker of God's laws. No one gets it right all the time. That's why marriage done right means an equal amount of forgiving and repenting.
I'm not sure to what extent *anger* figured into my grief, but it's a big factor for many people.

After her husband died, my friend Jude was so consumed by anger over mistreatment from him and the financial mess he had left behind, she knew she had to do something. "I got two boxes," she said. "I marked one 'anger' and the other 'thanksgiving.' Every time I got angry at Bob for something, I wrote it on a slip of paper and dropped it into that box. Then, I made myself write out two things for which I was thankful and put them into their box." She had intended to do something important with them, Jude said, like have a bonfire for the box of angry memos. "But Katrina took care of that." Her home was destroyed by the hurricane of 2005.

Fear was a small element in my grief. How would I be able to manage without my wife? And what if something else should happen now, if someone else dear to me were to die? How could I handle another unexpected tragedy? I was completely drained, with no resources in reserve. Another tragedy would be the worst thing imaginable. I thought of how in 2005, after Hurricane Katrina devastated the Mississippi Gulf Coast and flooded New Orleans where I was director of missions for Southern Baptist churches, our misery was compounded by the fear that another storm on the heels of that one would ruin the city forever. Thank the Lord, no hurricane has battered the city since the big one.

****

In this little collection of thoughts and suggestions, we will try to point the reader to that One variously called the Resurrection and the Life, the Author and Finisher of our faith, and the Bright and Morning Star.

It's all about Jesus, from the first to the last.

Simon Peter said it as well as it can be said. "Lord, to whom (else) shall we go? Thou hast the words of eternal life" (John 6:68).

Where indeed? The old gospel song asked, "Where could I go but to the Lord?"

Perhaps our answer is not unlike the fellow who was told by our Lord that all things are possible if he would believe. "Lord," the man said, "I believe; help my unbelief" (Mark 9:24).

Jesus did. He honored such an honest prayer.

He will help us. He loves to assist the seeking, hurting soul who will humble themselves before Him. When a leper fell at His feet, saying, "Lord, if you are willing, you can make me clean," Jesus did the unthinkable and touched the untouchable. "I am willing," He said.

The man became whole.

He is every bit as willing to help us.

Ladies and gentlemen, we have a Savior, His name is Jesus, and there is no One else like Him.

PART 2

Coping: What to do now?

(aka, Steps to dealing with grief)

When I was a young teen, my grandmother's brother died. As people did in those days, the extended family and friends overflowed their little home the evening before the funeral. Food was everywhere and each room crowded with people talking. To this day, I can hear my Aunt Carrie weeping over the death of her husband. She cried out into the crowded house, "What am I going to do now? How will I ever live without his precious arms holding me in the middle of the night?"

In my youthfulness, I was embarrassed by that tiny glimpse into their intimacy and surprised by her raw pain. It was a reality I knew nothing about.

Her question--"What am I going to do now?"--is faced by everyone who loses a loved one in death.

No one has all the answers. But Bertha and I can share what we have gone through and a couple of things we learned.

Here are our suggestions on what to do after the funeral, when we return to the house suddenly made emptier than we ever thought possible....

Step One: We can cry.

Go ahead and weep. If there ever was a time for unleashing your emotions, this is it.

Not only is it okay to cry, it's important to do so.

After all, you've just had an amputation.

You've just lost a part of yourself.

It hurts like crazy.

When I was a kid on the Alabama farm, I loved to walk through the woods and wade the streams and explore the hills and hollows. Sometimes I would come across a small sapling with a large vine wrapping around it. The two were so entwined, they seemed to be one. At least once, out of curiosity perhaps, I cut the vine at the base and unstripped it from around the tree. What was left was large indentations and ruts circling the length of the small tree where the vine had lived and grown.

That naked tree was me without my wife.

So I cried.

Over the six days she lingered in the ICU, I would stand by her bed for hours holding her hand. Sometimes I wept, sometimes I sang hymns, and sometimes recited scripture or prayed. "Honey," I said to her, "you would be so surprised at how much I'm crying. I can't seem to stop."

In some ways, it felt good to cry. When the tears were gone and no more would come, I felt empty and drained, but cleansed.

Our Lord wept. Not only at the famous scene at the tomb of Lazarus (John 11:35), but at other times. Hebrews 5:7 says, "In the days of His flesh, He offered up prayers and supplications with loud crying and tears...."

I am well aware that not everyone has tears and that people handle these things in different ways. One grieving the loss of a loved one should not inflict further pain on themselves by feeling guilty that the tears are not flowing. Most will cry later when friends have departed and the reality sets in.

David said, "Put thou my tears in thy bottle" (Psalm 56:8). Whatever else that means, it surely says our tears are precious to the Father, as they should be to us.

So, when the urge comes to weep, the safe choice is always to let the tears go and not try to hold them back.

Step Two: We can believe God.

We can trust the One who died for us. When He gave the wonderful promises of John 14 ("Let not your heart be troubled.... In my Father's house are many mansions.... I will come again and receive you unto myself...."), Jesus said, "If it were not so, I would have told you."

He keeps His promises. His character is on the line here. His faithfulness is what matters.

At no time is our faith in Jesus Christ more important than now. At no time is our faith more tested than now, when one dear to us has been taken.

You can believe Jesus. When He spoke of eternal things to Nicodemus (John chapter 3), Jesus paused to assure Him of one overriding reason why He could be trusted in such matters. "No one has been to Heaven," He said, "except the One who came from there, even the Son of Man," referring to Himself.

Jesus is a native of Heaven. He knows. Everyone else who ever wrote or spoke of Heaven was citing some other authority or telling a revelation they had received. But when Jesus spoke of Heaven, He was talking about His homeland. He is our Authority on Heaven.

It's all about Jesus.

The Apostle Paul said, "For if we believe that Jesus died and rose again, even so also will God bring with Him those who sleep in Jesus" (I Thessalonians 4:14).

It's important to make a distinction between believing Jesus and *feeling* something. The Lord's faithfulness is not dependent on our feeling anything. There is no way to emphasize this too strongly.

Many of God's children have bought into the lie that they have to feel a thing before it is true. And if they are not feeling it, then it's not there. They did not get this from Holy Scripture, because it's not taught there. Emotions are fickle and undependable. They are not to be trusted.

In 1997, my grandson was almost three. My journal records this from him: "Grant said, 'Grandpa, I would like to ride in a plane with you and Grandma and go see Uncle Marty and Aunt Misha." I told him that would be fine, that we could do that. Then he said, "I would hold on real tight."

The understanding of a child is a wonder, isn't it? In time, Grant would take many plane flights and would learn that "holding on real tight" has nothing to do with anything.

And so with the things of God. God is faithful. He is our keeper. A hundred times or more Scripture says things like "He that keepeth Israel will neither slumber nor sleep" (Psalm 121:3) and He is "my refuge and my fortress" (Psalm 91:2).

The Lord Jesus said, "I give unto them eternal life, and they shall never perish; and no one shall snatch them out of My hand." He added, "My Father, who has given them to Me, is greater than all, and no one is able to snatch them out of the Father's hand' (John 10:28-29). Nothing could be clearer than this.

He "holds us real tight."

And so, you and I who grieve will sit back and leave the matter to the Lord in whom we trust. How we feel has nothing to do with anything. What counts is His faithfulness.

Step Three: We can pray.

Talk to the Lord. If there was ever a time for seeking the help of the Savior, this is it. Even when you don't feel like praying, tell Him that.

Whether you call it prayer, or just unloading or venting, tell the Father what's on your heart.

Tell Him what's going on, how you feel, what you need. Ask Him your questions. Give Him your pain.

Give Him your faith, even when you feel it's so weak as to be almost non-existent. Mustard-seed faith will work just fine (Luke 17:6).

"Thank you, Lord." That three-word prayer may be as powerful as any it's possible to utter. Many a time in the hospital room when the patient was unable to speak, I've whispered that prayer and urged them to pray it continually. Sometimes when I have returned, the patient has held up three fingers to assure me they are praying our little prayer of thanksgiving.

If the patient improves and we are able to have a conversation in a subsequent visit, I remind them of the three dimensions of that prayer. We are thanking the Lord for what He has done in the *past*, what He is doing in the *present*, and all that He will do for us in the *future*. And yet, "thank you, Lord" sums it all up.

And when we don't feel like praying, it's all right to tell Him that, too.

God is never offended by our honesty. Years ago, I heard of a fellow who was a big shot in his local church, who loved to parade his religion and enjoyed being called on to lead in public prayer. The man had cobbled together bits and parts of great prayers he had heard over the years, and as a result each prayer he offered was a work of art. Then one day, his child died. In his pain and anger, the man walked outside his house, shook his fist toward the heavens, and cursed God.

The narrator said that was the first prayer that man had ever uttered.

We're not really praying at all until we get honest with God.

Jesus said worship must always be "in spirit and in truth" (John 4:24). Whatever else that means, it surely is saying the worshiper must be honest with the Lord.

We should never fear offending God.

I love the reminder of Psalm 103:14. "He Himself knows our frame; He is mindful that we are but dust." The One who made us knows we are made of humble stuff. God is under no illusion about us. He knows He got no bargain when He saved us. When we fall, the only one surprised is us.

He welcomes our prayers.

Step Four: We can read scripture.

As much as you can, as often as possible, go to your Bible.

If there was ever a time for opening God's Word and listening to His voice, this is it.

God talks to us from the Scripture.

Veteran disciples of Jesus probably need no help in finding passages that speak to you and nurture your soul. However, no one knows all the Scripture. We appreciate friends pointing out passages that blessed them during their valleys. Before listing our favorites, let's make a few observations on getting the most from our Bibles during our time of hurt and pain.

--While reading a verse here and a verse there has its place, God's people do better focusing on a longer passage, a full chapter or more. Within these, we may be drawn to a smaller portion, a verse or a sentence perhaps, that will speak to us in a particular way. But focusing on the larger passage will keep us balanced and help our interpretation to stay in line.

--Scripture urges us to meditate on God's Word (See Psalm 1:2). The idea is to read something several times until we "have it," then reflect on it again and again over the next few days. Then, we return to it and read it again, this time studying the larger passage surrounding it. In all of this, we are listening for God to speak to us from His Word.

--Someone wonders how they will recognize the voice of the Lord when He does speak to them from His word. The best answer I know is simply, you will know. When a truth grasps your heart, but you know this is not your own doing, and when it is so right for the situation and so strong in your spirit, you may conclude this is the Lord Himself addressing His child. While we should be honored that He would deign to do such a wonderful thing as speak to us, we should not be surprised. Jesus said His sheep hear His voice and follow Him. (See John 10, particularly verses 1-30.)

Here are some passages we have come to hold dear...

--The Four Gospels contain almost all there is of the story of Jesus and His earthly ministry. Simply by reading it and letting His words soak into our hearts, we are instructed and our spirits are lifted. The lazy, carnal spirit within us may insist that "I know that story; I've read it a hundred times." But it's lying. The fact is there are more riches to be discovered in familiar Bible stories than most of us have ever imagined. Only those who sit at the feet of Jesus, so to speak, and remain there to listen to Him quietly and reflectively, only they will receive the special comfort He has for us.

--Of the Four Gospels, Luke seems to speak to the hurting soul best of all, in our opinion. This Gospel has a special word for children, women, the oppressed, the persecuted, the hurting.

--All the Psalms, but these in particular: Psalms 1, 23, 27, 37, 40, 51, 59, 66, 71, 73, 84, and 91.

Let's pause here to say a word about the Psalms. When I was a young pastor, this collection of Hebrew songs had little appeal for me. As I aged, and as life handed me lesson after lesson on suffering, I began to see them as the treasure they are. But not everything in all the 150 Psalms will speak to every believer. The Spirit does not do a one-size-fits-all ministry, but speaks to us as the individuals He has made us to be. So, it's good to read the Psalms with a highlighter or a fine-point pen (or to keep a notebook handy) and make notes of the special verses or sentences that seem to have our names on them.

My friend Robby: "The best way I know to receive comfort in my grief is to worship God in the midnight hours. I urge you to read the Psalms. Cry the Psalms."

--From the epistles, we particularly recommend Romans 8, I Corinthians 13, 2 Corinthians 5, Philippians 4, and Colossians 1.

Step Five: We can give thanks.

You can always find reasons to give thanks.

The day Margaret took her last breath, I came home and cleaned out her room. Later that night I wrote in my journal:

I spent a couple of hours cleaning the bedroom where Margaret had been sleeping because of her illness. I removed all the medicines, the pamphlets on this condition or that program, the reading materials, the tissues, and a hundred other things. When I picked up the folder reading "Crohn's & Colitis," as I tossed it in the trash, I called out, "Goodbye, Crohn's Disease! Goodbye Colitis! Goodbye knee pain! Goodbye weight problems! Goodbye depression! The former things have passed away! He shall wipe away all tears from their eyes! No more suffering, no more death. He makes all things new! Praise God from whom all blessings flow!"

As I collapsed into tears, the Lord and I had an old-fashioned revival meeting right there on the carpet.

As much as anything, I gave thanks (then, and still do now) she was out of the pain and misery she had lived with the last decade of her life. Many a time when she was weeping from the torture, Margaret would say something like, "If I knew it would not hurt my loved ones so much, I would end my own life."

I would not bring her back to that for anything.

Even now, over two years later, I cannot type this without the tears flowing.

I made a discovery about the overcoming power thanksgiving after my dad went to Heaven in 2007. When my heart would be hurting so badly for him, if I began to think about all I was thankful for--what he had taught me, the fun we had had, dad's sacrifice for his family over the decades, etc.--the pain went away. Discovering this was like finding gold. From then on, my pain gave way to thanksgiving.

Evidently, grief and thanksgiving do not coexist very well. I have no idea why. I'm a pastor not a mental health expert. A witness, not an analyst.

Scripture seems to hint at this. "Be anxious for nothing, but in everything with prayer and supplication *with thanksgiving* let your requests be known unto God. And the peace of God which passes understanding will keep your hearts and minds in Christ Jesus" (Philippians 4:6).

In my journal, I listed a number of reasons I had to be thankful after my wife's death....

1) Margaret was not driving when she collapsed.

We've all heard of drivers passing out and crashing into other vehicles and taking out whole families. That could easily have happened.

2) The salon was one block from the police station and a half-mile from the fire department. When she collapsed, help arrived as quickly as we could ever have asked.

3) I'm thankful we had enjoyed an hour at the breakfast table that morning.

4) I'm grateful she was being proactive about all the health issues she was facing. She was a fighter, not one to give up, although the temptation to throw in the towel was ever present.

5) Over Christmas holidays, just one month earlier, two of our three Missouri granddaughters came to visit. Margaret and I drove them across the lake to the English Tea Room at Covington. She had a great time. Then, just after Christmas, our Carolina son arrived with his family for a few days of love and laughter. So, we have much to be thankful for.

Giving thanks helps me deal with the overwhelming pain of missing my wife. When I start telling the Heavenly Father ways in which she blessed me and praising Him for His goodness, the pain disappears.

So far, I'm up to blessing number seven thousand thirty five.

None of this is meant to imply that one session of thanksgiving banishes grief forever. The loss of our loved one will always be a reality in our lives and the pain will never completely go away. And in a very real sense, that's all right. We do not ever want to *not* miss this one we hold so dear, who meant so much to us.

Those who know the Lord, we're told, never see each other for the last time. Believers have so much for which to give thanks.

Step Six: We can get up and do something.

Stay busy doing the essentials, the really important things.

If in the evening your wife died, in the morning do as the Lord commanded. That's Ezekiel 24:18.

Years ago, the wonderful Elisabeth Elliot, missionary in her own right and widow of martyred missionary Jim Elliot, taught an important lesson on this. When depressed--and we find it encouraging that even the great ones undergo the same trials in life the rest of us do!--she would not feel like making big decisions, she said. She taught herself to get up and "do the next thing."

Mrs. Elliot said she might get up from her couch and go toss in a load of washing. Then, she would sweep the porch. After that, she might iron the handkerchiefs. One thing after another. What she did not do was make a long list of jobs to tackle throughout the day. Her depression would not allow that. But by "doing the next thing," at the end of the day she had accomplished a great deal.

She had not given in to her depression.

For those who grieve and cannot see beyond the next hour, we may choose simply to do the next thing, at least until we feel strong enough to make bigger plans and embrace larger projects.

A few days after my wife's homegoing, I was back in the pulpit preaching. A month later, I flew to California and spent several days with pastors in a retreat setting not far from Yosemite.

Staying busy in the work of the Lord was the best thing I could have done.

About that time, I wrote in my journal:

Last night late, I got out of bed and wrote down something the Holy Spirit was saying to me. The note reads:

"Her work was done, but mine goes on."

And what work is that? I wrote this down:

"Preach the Word. Love my family. Write these books. Draw some cartoons. Encourage the faithful. Witness to the others. Give to the needy.

"Repeat as necessary."

To stay with the calling of God on our life is the main thing.

Step Seven: We can humble ourselves before God.

We will need to do it again tomorrow, and the day after.

He is Lord and we're not. And that's just fine.

We must guard against thinking the Lord owes us anything. We must shield ourselves against the temptation to think God was punishing us by taking our loved one.

We humans are pretty amazing in our ability to read offense into everything we find painful.

From one end to the other, Scripture tells us to humble ourselves. The best way to do that, I expect, is by focusing on the greatness of the Lord and the majesty of His universe. (Psalm 8 is a prime example.)

Some people pray, "Lord, humble us." But Scripture tells us to humble ourselves.

In the Bible, when God humbled someone, He did it with a heavy hand (See Daniel 4:30ff). Some did not survive the experience (See Acts 12:20ff for the fatal humbling of a proud king).

Much better to humble ourselves.

The Apostle Paul urges, "Through the grace given to me I say to every man among you not to think more highly of himself than he ought to think, but to think so as to have sound judgment, as God has allotted to each a measure of faith" (Romans 12:3). Along the same lines, the Psalmist prayed, "Keep back thy servant from presumptuous sins" (Psalm 19:14). We are presumptuous when we become self-important and believe God owes us anything.

Finding the balance between exaggerating our importance and undermining our self-respect is a constant struggle for many, but absolutely essential if we are to function well in this world.

All of life is a gift from God. He owes us nothing. And yet, listening to people vent their anger at Him for taking their loved one, one would think God had violated an agreement or reneged on a promise.

Being human, we may tend to assume we will be given long lives and that our loved ones will always be with us. So, when a life is cut short prematurely--by our way of measurement, let us emphasize--it's natural to hurt and to feel short-changed by the Almighty.

"The Lord giveth, the Lord taketh away," said the bereaved Job after burying all ten of his children. "Blessed be the name of the Lord." (Job 1:21)

That praise, quoted so often by God's children over the centuries, stands as the gold standard for how to respond when the Father takes from us one who is as dear as life itself.

The Psalmist helps. "Know that the Lord Himself is God. It is He who has made us and not we ourselves.

We are His people and the sheep of His pasture" (Psalm 100:3).

Do the sheep dictate to the shepherd? Do they criticize him when he doesn't lead them in the way they had planned? Do they rebel and demand another shepherd when they don't get the pasture they'd requested or the rest they feel they deserve?

All of life belongs to the Creator. Does the painting talk back to the artist? The sculpted piece sass the sculptor?

And yet, we talk back to our Heavenly Father.

Humility does not come naturally to us. We seem to arrive fresh from the womb with an inborn sense of entitlement. Perhaps that's the notorious original sin we hear so much about.

We are the Lord's workmanship, Scripture says (Ephesians 2:10). We depend on Him for the very air we breathe. To dictate anything to the Creator God is ludicrous.

We are such finite, limited, helpless beings. And the sooner we realize that, the quicker we can throw ourselves on His mercy and find that "His strength is made perfect in our weakness," and "when I am weak, then am I strong." (2 Corinthians 12) Only those who humble themselves before Him and put their trust in

Him will ever see this; to everyone else, it will be incomprehensible and just so much foolishness.

Step Eight: We can remember!

Think of the wonderful times you had, the things your loved one said and did which blessed you so much.

The best feature of a good funeral--is that an oxymoron?--is often tributes from friends and loved ones.

--"I remember the time we..."

--"One thing he said that will always stay with me...."

--"I was telling someone the other day of the time when we...."

My friend Cindy said, "I gave people permission to talk and mention my daddy's name. So many people don't know what to say, but I want you to tell me something I may not have known about him."

When Air Force Captain Robert Boland died in the crash of his jet, at the funeral in our church, two of his Academy classmates told of Robert witnessing to them of his Christian faith. Nothing was more comforting to his family than that.

When Emmalee Holland died, at her funeral the minister told how she had said in the hospital, "I must be a lot sicker than I thought. Everyone who comes in here tells me how much they love me!" We all laughed. It sounded like something she would say.

At Ed Logan's funeral, the minister told how on the last day of his life, Ed attended a meeting of the Gideons to discuss getting the Word of God into the schools and jails. An hour later, he had breakfast with his wife Mary Ellen. Up in the morning, he was plowing his neighbor's garden when a heart attack took him. "What a way to go," said the preacher. Indeed.

Following Margaret's funeral, our church provided a luncheon in the fellowship hall with an open microphone set up for those who wished to speak. My roommate during college told how he alerted me to Margaret, and how dense I was until the chemistry kicked in! Joel Davis then went on to become my best man (as well as a lifelong encourager). Not all the stories were spiritual. (smiley-face goes here.) Friends Jim and Darlene Graham and daughter Brandy had driven over from Atlanta. Darlene, who attended college with my wife, said, "Maggie taught me it's all right to say 'damn.'" The room exploded with laughter--and gave us the lift we so badly needed.

When people say, "I will never forget the time..." everything inside you goes on full alert. Hearing a story about your beloved is better medicine and greater therapy than anything the professionals can offer at any price.

Step Nine: We can make some important choices.

You can't do everything, but you can do some things. Leave the rest until later.

Recently, a tornado ripped through Hattiesburg, Mississippi and killed several people in addition to doing millions of dollars of damage. Later, our Jackson newspaper carried interviews with the families of the four people who were killed.

The widow of a 58-year-old man who was killed said, "That was a bad day. But I'm choosing which battles to fight. Some of them I can, some of them I can't. The majority of them I can't."

She continued, "I'm choosing to fight the battle of picking up the pieces--that's the only one I can deal with right now."

We make choices every day of our lives, good times and bad.

My friend Carla said, "It's important to stay connected with people. And make your bed so you won't be tempted to crawl back in to avoid the world. If you get nothing else done that day, at least you made your bed!"

Dr. Larry Kennedy gave me a story about choices.

His son Steve, age 7, was attending his first big-church wedding. He sat in the church sanctuary beside his mother and watched as the door in front opened and his father entered, followed by seven handsome young men dressed in their tuxedos. They lined across the front, a handsome lot. Then, the bridesmaids entered. As the bride slowly moved down the aisle on the arm of her father, little Steve tugged on his mom's arm and said, "Mother. Does she already know which one of those men she's going to marry? Or is she going to decide when she gets down there?"

Larry Kennedy added, "We can save ourselves a lot of pain later in life by making some choices early."

We cannot do everything, nor should we. The common wisdom is that the widowed should make no big decisions--such as selling the house and moving, or remarrying--for the first year. That seems to be wise.

Step Ten: We can read.

So many helpful books and articles have been written by people who have been where you find yourself today.

When we began to make a list of books on grief we found helpful, things got complicated. Some books are better than others, some we found a little help in, but not much. One or two with helpful insights had questionable theology.

44

Eventually, Bertha suggested that a better course may be simply to ask someone you trust to recommend a good book. So--other than this one! (smile, please)--we won't be listing books.

Your church library--I sure hope you have access to a good one--should have a nice collection of books on grief.

Another resource is pastors and counselors who deal with people trying to recover from their grief. Most will have good reading material and can recommend other books and pamphlets.

If you can, walk into a Lifeway Christian Store and ask a clerk to point you to books on grief. Stand there and read the first chapters of several, then make your selections.

After you find books that help, keep them close so you can share them with friends experiencing the same life-altering loss you have gone through. Don't worry about not getting the books back. You don't want them back. As you hand the book to a friend, emphasize, "I don't want it back." That will free them from the guilt we have all felt over borrowed books--which we didn't ask for in the first place and can't remember who lent them to us!

My friend Bruce Fields reads a book, then passes it on. That way, he says, he does not end up with stacks of books for which he has no further use. Bruce blesses a lot of people in this way.

Step Eleven: We can laugh.

Give yourself permission to laugh. Laughter is medicine for a sad soul.

In 2004-05, after the doctor removed a cancer from the underside of my tongue, I endured several months of radiation of the head and neck area. That was a miserable period of my life, I will admit, but the good news is the cancer never reappeared and we're now going on 13 years. However...

When the effects of the radiation were at their worst, my mouth had blisters, food had lost its taste, and my energy level was non-existent. So, each morning after returning home from the radiation center, I would pull a Reader's Digest off the shelf and read all the marked passages. For several years prior to that time, as soon as the newest issue of RD appeared, I would go through and read the stories and jokes and circle in bold ink those I liked best.

I had no idea how that would come in so handy.

That was the only laughter I found in the months of radiation therapy.

I recommend laughter. If necessary, volunteer in the church nursery and surround yourself with small children for an hour or two each week. Their sweet spirits will lift yours.

Norman Cousins is famous for his book, "Anatomy of an Illness," on the healing power of laughter. (His story is easily located in Wikipedia and other places.) In essence, he discovered the healing power of endorfins, the chemical released by the brain as a result of prolonged deep laughter. Cousins would watch reruns of television comedies and tapes of Marx Brothers movies and laugh himself silly. As a result, his vital signs improved for a period. Then, his wife would replay the favorite episodes and he would laugh again, and the positive signs would reappear.

Eventually, Cousins got well and wrote his book.

We can all recall spending an evening with old friends, during which we laughed and reminisced and had a great time. At the end of the evening, our faces were flushed, our spirits were elated, the adrenalin was pumping, and we felt better than we had in years. Those who study such things tell us it's the endorfins at work. Nature's healers. Nature's high.

Sometimes in conferences on laughter, I urge the participants to simply make themselves laugh nonstop for 45 seconds. It's easy to do, I tell them, and then demonstrate it. The pure silliness of the exercise is fun and soon people are giggling and pointing at each other and teasing one another. Laughter is wonderful medicine, even when we make ourselves do it.

"Thou hast put gladness in my heart, more than when their grain and new wine increased" (Psalm 4:7). And then, the best one of all...

"God has made laughter for me" (Genesis 21:6).

God has made laughter for each of us. Some of us, I fear, are not getting our minimum daily requirement.

Step Twelve: We can journal.

Get a wordless book and start writing.

I was a journaler for a long time. In 1990, I found myself between churches--an awkward time for any pastor--and decided the time would come when I would wonder what was going on then, what was I thinking and feeling. So, I bought a hard-bound wordless book, wrote the date in the front and began writing.

I had no idea that I would end up chronicling the entire decade of the 1990s, filling over 50 of these books.

There's something special about putting pen to paper and writing. I am well aware we have the computer and it's so much more convenient. This book is being written on my ASUS laptop. Even so, most people will find the actual handwriting of a journal therapeutic.

What to do? Buy a wordless, hardbound book at any bookstore. Get an ink pen of some kind, put the date at the top of the page, and begin writing.

What should you write? Anything you wish. It's your book and presumably no one else will ever see it but you. It's not a diary, but a journal, a record of this day. You might write in it--

--what you are thinking and feeling today.

--anything that happened today, who called on you, what their visit meant.

--events or calls or notes or contacts of any kind that you found interesting or helpful or offensive or divine.

--anything you will want to remember later. Scriptures, prayers, something you read.

Step Thirteen: We can reach out and help someone.

It may or may not be someone who has lost a loved one in death. Simply reaching out to a person in need blesses the giver as much as the recipient.

Every church office will have the names of needy people in the area who could use a helping hand. Charitable agencies are always looking for volunteers. A Sunday School class may have members who need a visit, a bag of groceries, or a ride to the doctor.

When we get out of our shell and help a brother or sister, we benefit more than they.

Somewhere, I heard of a proposed grief ministry where the organizers planned to pull the grieving into classes for a number of weeks, then send them out to target others like themselves with a plan for so-many visits and ministries.

While the organizers were doubtless well-intentioned, they were missing a huge fact: People grieve in different ways. When reeling from the death of a spouse or child, most people have no desire to join a regimented plan calling for a full schedule of meetings and ministries. I imagine the leaders found that out when they tried putting their plan into effect.

Even so, the person overcome with sadness at the loss of someone special will do well to look around for a person in need--any kind of need--and lend a hand. The wonderful story in Matthew 25:31ff reminds us of the high value our Lord places on our efforts to feed the hungry, give water to the thirsty, clothe the naked, etc.

Step Fourteen: We can get outside and take a walk.

Bertha and I are walkers. We have each walked for many years, and continue to do so now.

She reminds me to say that for those who have not been walking at all, short jaunts are better at first.

Walking, they tell us, is the best all-around exercise. It activates all kinds of muscles and various organs. People who walk tend to have fewer health problems, more energy, and to live longer.

There's no way to know for sure, but walking could be the best explanation for Bertha and I being in our late 70's and still enjoying great health.

My journal of the decade of the 1990s records how night after night, I walked two or three or four miles in the neighborhood or on a path through the park. I was doing it for my health, yes, but for a hundred other reasons. As a pastor of a church recovering from a huge split, often I was experiencing stress and pressure from a number of directions. Walking gave me the opportunity to be alone, to think things through, to talk out matters, and to pray. To this day, I love to walk and pray.

Walking is better than jogging. Most of the joggers I know have had knee problems. But with walking, one

51

has time to enjoy nature, to actually see what's going on around you, and to talk to the Lord.

For pastors, the daily walk is a great time to go over sermons. Talking the messages out quietly enables the preacher to test his understanding of the text, to see whether his explanation works or is a dead-end path, and to test-drive his story-telling.

A friend laughs at the counsel I once gave him. Now, let me say that I remember none of it. But my friend Larry said once when he was depressed and we were chatting, I asked if he walked. "I do," he said, "a couple of miles a day." And he says I asked, "What do you do while you're walking?" He answered, "I go over my schedule, think about what I did that day and need to get right tomorrow. I make plans for the next day." Larry says that I told him, "That's the dumbest thing I ever heard of!"

According to his account, I counseled him to spend the time talking to the Lord, praising Him right out of Scripture or with hymns, and then unburdening himself with whatever he was dealing with at the moment. "Talk to the Lord! Tell Him what's going on. Give Him the chance to get into that mess with you!"

I seriously doubt I was that blunt, but the counsel is something I believe in strongly.

Scripture tells us that Jesus was known to get up early and walk in the mountains talking to the Father (see

Mark 1:35). Of course, as the Lord and His disciples walked from town to town during their ministry, the conversations they held along the way--each of them talking and listening--were precisely the kind of thing we want to do today. Walk with Jesus, talk with Him, and then be quiet and listen.

Step Fifteen: We can get a dog.

That counsel--"Get a dog!"--was given by a realtor to Bertha and her family when their children had grown up and left home, and she and Gary had moved to a new church. Walking a dog is a great way to meet one's neighbors, said the realtor.

When people stop on the street to remark on the pet, such conversations often develop into friendships.

My sister Carolyn has no children but three dogs whom she loves dearly. Dogs give unconditional love in a way few humans can. Of course, they have to be taken outside for regular walks. But for someone who wants to retreat into the house and never emerge again-- someone dealing with grief, for instance--this can be a lifesaver.

My first experience with a house dog is occurring as we speak. When Bertha and I married, she brought with her Albie, a mixed breed Sheltie, as gentle and beautiful and sweet as any animal ever. I quickly began to share the responsibility for his care, and as he warmed to me discovered that I adore this little dog.

People who know about these things suggest you not rush into getting a dog without doing the necessary preparation, reading up, etc. Some dogs work better than others for the grieving. A few days ago as I write, while preaching in a church in East Tennessee, we had dinner one evening after church with a family with two Great Danes *in the house*. They were the size of young horses! Now, that would not work for me, thank you. Something slightly larger than a house cat is about all I can deal with.

I can see how the elderly in nursing homes would respond to visits from a loving pet. Their sweetness touches something inside us that few other things can.

A good way to find out if you want a dog or can deal with the requirements would be to volunteer to dog-sit a friend's pet for a day or two, just to try it out. When the family has to go out of town, boarding the dog in a kennel can be costly. So, if you were to volunteer to keep the family pet for a weekend, you would be doing your friends a favor and giving yourself the opportunity to find out if this is for you.

Friends suggest you check out your local animal shelter before going further. See what is available at little to no cost. Ask around, go online, do your homework. It could be one of the best things you could ever do for yourself.

Step Sixteen: We can practice self-talk.

Sometimes we need to give ourselves a "good talking-to!"

That practice--talking straight to oneself--occurs all through Scripture.

When the Psalmist says something like "O my soul," he's calling on himself to get his act together and to start blessing God.   The wonderful 103rd Psalm starts and ends with those words.

I love the way the Psalmist said it in Psalm 116:7. "Return to your rest, O my soul, for the Lord hath dealt bountifully with you." He's telling anxiety to "get back in your hole, because the Lord has shown Himself so faithful in the past, we should not hesitate to trust Him with our future."

Sports fans will see football coaches ream out a player on the sideline, sometimes with harsh language. A wise coach will know which player needs strong talk and which ones respond best to soft words. In talking to ourselves, my hunch is strong words work better than the gentler kind.

Dieters standing before the refrigerator have been known to talk to themselves, with something like "Do you really need that?" or "Are you really hungry?" and "Come on, Jack! No food tastes as good as slim feels!"

Someone once prayed, "Lord, give me a heart of fire toward Thee, a heart of flesh toward others, and a heart of iron toward myself." The idea is not to be too soft on oneself, not to indulge our desire for ease and comfort, but to become strong and disciplined and tough on ourselves at the same time we are compassionate toward other people and devoted to the Savior.

Step Seventeen: We can rejoice. Sing even.

I can hear someone saying, "I feel like I'm dying and you tell me to rejoice?" And, "I don't feel like rejoicing."

These are the very people who need to be rejoicing and expressing their praise to the loving Heavenly Father.

Someone says, "But if I don't feel it, to do it would be fake." We answer, "No, it would be faith."

Somewhere along the way, many of us have convinced ourselves that our feelings are what authenticates our actions. We must feel love before expressing it, feel gratitude before writing a thank-you note, or feel happy before singing.

And if we are not feeling something, to do it anyway would be hypocrisy.

Nothing could be further from the truth.

"We walk by faith, not by sight" (2 Corinthians 5:7).

To do anything by faith means there are positive and negative aspects to the action. The positive is simply that "I believe in the Heavenly Father, in the Lord Jesus Christ!" The negative is the "however" aspect. There are some difficulties. Those difficulties may be a lack of resources, or the presence of obstacles, illness, or pain. "Abraham went out not knowing where he was going," says Hebrews 11:8.

At the end of Luke 18 and the start of the next chapter, we see two men acting on faith to get to Jesus. The blind beggar of Jericho, named Bartimaeus in Mark 10, kept calling for Jesus when people urged him to be quiet. The diminutive tax collector of the same city climbed a tree in order to see Jesus when crowds were blocking the way.

They believed, but there were difficulties.

To praise God in the midst of our pain is a wonderful expression of faith. We can see a vivid demonstration in Acts 16:25. Paul and Silas had been beaten and jailed for nothing more than preaching the gospel. In their great pain and discomfort, "about midnight they began to pray and sing hymns of praise to God."

We can be sure they did not feel like singing. Yet, they were expressing their love for the Lord and their confidence that He was in charge and was using this awful situation for His purposes. As He surely did.

So, go ahead and rejoice in the Lord by faith. And while you're at it, do whatever is necessary to rescue your spiritual life from bondage to your emotions. "Without faith, it is impossible to please God" (Hebrews 11:6).

Jann told me, "I sing out loud the hymns that have sustained me. 'Great is Thy Faithfulness' and 'It is Well With My Soul.' I can still hear my Dad singing in the hallway of our home, 'Jesus is All the World To Me.' My mom's favorites were 'One Day at a Time' and 'My Faith Looks Up to Thee.' These hymns have lifted me to joyful song, encouraged me, quietened me, and kept me grounded in multiple ways."

Step Eighteen: Do a memorial.

A book of mom's recipes. A quilt made up of her dresses. Put his sermons on CDs.

After Margaret's death, a friend whom I had not met invited us to send her dresses which she would turn into a quilt. A few months later, here came this amazing gift in the mail, large enough for the king-sized bed. (The friend insisted this was a gift, but since it had taken so many hours--days and weeks!--of her time, I sent her a check and made her a cartoon thank-you note.)

My friend Ferebe said, "When my mother died, I decided to make the anniversary of her death each year a celebration, not a day of mourning. When Gary and

I married, he took up the mantle and named February 1 "Oma Day." He buys us yellow roses that day, one for her grave and the rest for our house."

Joni lists quite a few suggestions, including "posting pictures of the loved one on social media, sharing anecdotes and her pain on Facebook with friends who prayed for me."

Joni is a writer, so she wrote the obituary for her loved one, and later a feature story.

She suggests putting together a memorial video of the loved one's life using photos and their favorite music.

She adds, "Do something that person loved to do. My mother and grandmother loved to cook--and taught me. So, I'm honoring them when I cook with my grandchildren."

My friend Diane says they took their mother's favorite recipes and published them in a book for family and friends.

Step Nineteen: We can see a counselor or join a group of fellow strugglers. They will understand.

Missie told us: "It took a Christian counselor to tell me God was big enough for my anger at Him for taking my brother from me. I was not raised to think in such a way, but realizing I could unleash all my hurt on my

Savior allowed me to let go and begin to heal. A week after this, the counselor encouraged me to ask God for healing, peace, and comfort. In both cases, God showed up in a big way. I was able to move forward with the anger and pain gone."

Margaret's therapist--another word for a counselor-- was Beverly, a trusted confidant whom she went to at varying times over a decade. So, twice after Margaret's death, I made appointments and talked with Beverly for an hour. She listened well, asked probing questions, and made helpful suggestions.

What I've discovered is that many Christian people are reluctant to call on a counselor. To them, this represents a failure of some kind, an admission that they have not found the strength in Christ they should have. This is foolish. They would not hesitate to check themselves into a hospital for an appendectomy or see the dentist for a root canal. But somehow, when we are brought down by the unexpected death of a beloved spouse or child or friend, we are supposed to bear this alone?

My experience with Beverly, a Roman Catholic, is that her faith in Christ is a huge part of her work as a counselor. I've referred church members to her when they struggled with an incorrigible child, a difficult family issue, or some inner turmoil that was beyond my ability as pastor to resolve.

Some of God's finest servants work, not behind a pulpit, but in the counseling office where they assist hurting people one at a time.

When I pastored, in referring someone to a counselor, if they were reluctant, I would encourage them to go once and try it. If it was not helpful or if for any reason they preferred another counselor, I would still be there to assist them. Almost invariably, they reported back favorable results.

A word about my own experience may be helpful. As a young husband pouring himself into the work of pastoring, I was in danger of neglecting my family. When Margaret suggested we go for counseling, I resisted. Finally, with my acquiescence, she went without me, and the improvement was immediate and enormous. So, at a later time, I began to accompany her. The counselor became a great friend. Thereafter I was sold on counseling.

Obviously, the most important thing is to find the right person to counsel. Pastors and trusted friends can help with this.

As for group therapy, the ministry most often mentioned by my friends is called **GriefShare**. Many people have found great strength in the relationships and exercises of such small group gatherings.

Compassionate Friends is a ministry conducted by people who have lost a child in death, reaching out to others like themselves. They emphasize that "child" does not have to refer to any particular age. When my youngest brother died, my mother, almost 90 years old, wrote in her Bible "the worst day of my life." To lose a child at any age can be devastating. We appreciate those who dedicate themselves to welcoming the hurting and giving them comfort.

Step Twenty: Write a long letter to your loved one.

My friend Nancy says this was a great help to her. She said, "My grief therapist suggested I write a long letter to my son, remembering all the good memories, including experiences and feelings of joy we shared. This was a year after his death, as a way of bringing some closure to my intense grief. It was very helpful to focus only on good experiences and happy feelings."

Nancy says she keeps the letter in her memory box, "right on top." Most years on the anniversary of her son's death, she goes there, reads the letter, and spends a few minutes reflecting on those good memories.

There is a custom in New Orleans, where we lived for nearly 27 years, which I find interesting. At certain times of the year, Mother's Day for instance, people take out newspaper ads to publish pictures of their deceased loved ones with a few words of devotion. At first, being the farm boy from Alabama, I found the custom strange. Did they think, I wondered, that their loved ones take the newspaper in Heaven? But over the years, I came to realize that posting a tribute to these special ones gave themselves comfort. And anything that gives comfort to the hurting is surely worth the few dollars for a newspaper ad.

As a pastor, when counseling with a bereaved family prior to the memorial service, I would encourage them to have a couple family members to share a tribute or offer a eulogy. And, many times, they would read a letter which they or a sibling had penned to their loved one. It never failed to be comforting.

Whether anyone else reads the letter or hears it read, one who is grieving the loss of a loved one would do well to take a few minutes (or as long as it takes!) to pen a note of love and remembrance. Then, the letter should be kept with other memorabilia and keepsakes.

Step Twenty-One : Ask your friends what helped them cope.

After her only sister went to Heaven, Becky Brown borrowed her Bible and took it home with her. She read it for months. Becky enjoyed the notes in the margin, and paid close attention to the underlined and highlighted passages.

Tom said, "I stroll around graveyards. Doing so reminds me that death comes to us all. Somehow it's helpful to walk through the cemetery, to read the stones, reflect, pray, and then walk out the gates. There's still work to do, but I am stronger and more focused from my interlude in the graveyard."

When Mr. C. C. Hope, Senior, died, in his 90s, his son shared a favorite story with me.

"My parents were married in 1919," he said. "After the wedding, my grandmother took the roses from Mom's bridal bouquet and put into a jar of water and rooted them. Then, she set them out in the yard. Over the years since, every bride in this family has carried roses from Mom's bridal bouquet."

He grew teary-eyed and said, "Pop is lying in the casket in the next room now, holding in his hands roses from his bride's wedding bouquet."

Ask your friends what they did. You might be blessed in unexpected ways.

PART 3

Bertha's story

Bertha Pepper married Dr. Gary Fagan in 1962. They became the parents of a daughter Lari and a son Jeff, and eventually grandparents of six wonderful young people. In ministry, they served churches in several states before going as missionaries to Africa and South America. Gary was called to Heaven in May, 2014. Below is Bertha's account of dealing with the death of her beloved husband. We chose the question and answer format...

1. Describe how you felt in the days following Gary's death.

Because expressing my feelings in writing has been an important daily routine for me for at least 40 years, I quickly sent the note below to the many friends we knew through the years and had stayed in contact with (personal friends, church members whom we pastored, and many friends in Malawi, Africa, and Brasilia, Brazil with whom we had worked as missionaries).

*My Message to Friends after Gary's Death:

Last night at 6:22 p.m., my precious husband Gary went to be with the Lord. My heart is so sad as I've been loved by him for almost 52 wonderful years   I just wanted you to know, so it is not as personal as I wanted it to be as time is very short and there is much to do.

Gary entered University Hospital's trauma unit, Critical Care Neuroscience, early Monday morning with a splitting headache. They found he had a bleed in the fourth ventricle of his brain. For several days, he seemed to be progressing well. Then on Friday evening, another stroke came. By Monday afternoon, the doctor told us there were no more options for treatment as Gary could not come back from the stroke in any way. We would need to let him go.

Gary and I had signed our Living Will several years ago, and we had talked about what each of us would want if such a situation should arise. In the past, Gary had always told me that he did not fear another heart attack or death as he knew he would be going Home to the Lord. However, he and I both feared another stroke that might leave him imprisoned in a body. In the hospital, Jeff, Lari, and I talked and prayed with Gary, played music for him that he had recorded on his phone—songs we all loved so much. I was able to lean my body over on Gary's chest all day and just listen to his heartbeat. Thus, I was able to hear the very last heartbeat, which I will treasure forever.

I hardly see how life can go on without my Gary, but I know it will and that the Lord will give our children and me strength and comfort for all the days ahead. I know where Gary is, and I believe that Heaven is all that the Bible tells us it is—and much, much more. Therefore, though I will grieve, I do not have to grieve as if I did not have the hope of seeing him again.

Thank you for all you have meant to us. I covet your fervent prayers.

A Few Days After, I wrote this:

*As all the books seem to tell us, everything is surreal, almost like this is happening to someone else. My mind and heart were numb. When her husband died, my sister Laura said, "It was like a movie that I was watching, but surely it could not be happening to me." This helped me to know I was "normal." I had decided years ago that when and if I should lose one of my precious family, I would not try to be the "perfect pastor's wife" and hide my grief, to be strong for everyone else--as a role model. So, when my time did come in Gary's death, I had a "plan," in a sense. I was able to release my emotions. Wonderful, long time friends came from long distances to surround and comfort me. Our children and grandchildren grieved together with me.

*One thing I found shocking, though. I had attended perhaps a thousand funerals with Gary as he preached comforting messages, and we surrounded friends as they went through the days, months and years of grieving the death of their loved ones. I thought I understood their grief. I was so wrong!! I had no idea of the depth of the huge, black hole that swallowed me and seemed not to let me go. For me, it was a life-saver to be able to share my feelings with close friends who loved, appreciated, and respected Gary and knew the person he really was.

*My family and friends who came for Gary's funeral finally had to leave. Though I did not feel like reading God's word, I knew it must have something for me. Sometimes I felt His Presence and sometimes He seemed far away; I had to rest on His promises that He really was there with me. The days ahead would be a complete blank if I had not consciously, just driven myself, to write my feelings in my journal daily as I had for so many years, telling the Lord about my sorrow, asking for His help. I continued my long practice of walking daily with my little dog for 30 minutes or so. Yes, I was just following advice that had seemed to help others.

My sister Laura was my greatest confidant. She lived close by, and she understood. She had lost her husband several years before and had loved him for 52 years also. Yet, it was a long, hard, uphill struggle to go from day to day. I could never imagine being able to laugh or enjoy life again. I continued to teach in a nearby college, which was a great help as I had to focus on students rather than myself--until I went back home to an empty house. I was glad that Gary and I had always had an inside dog. Our Sheltie, Corona, was comforting and was always ready for a walk. It would be a year and a half, though, before I found I no longer dreaded going home due to the pain.

* Sometime after Gary's death, I came to realize I did not know who I was. For 52 years, I had been a beloved wife; I had been a pastor's wife, a role which I always treasured. My world revolved around these. Now, who was I? What was my identity? I felt like what scripture records Naomi saying after her husband and sons had died in Moab and she was returning to Bethlehem. "Don't call me Naomi. Call me Mara (Naomi means pleasant; Mara means bitter). . . .I went out full and the Lord has brought me home empty." (Ruth 1:20-21) My life had been so full; now I was empty.

*There were painful decisions to be made. Our small church, which Gary began to pastor after we retired from overseas ministry, would need to look for another pastor. I went back a couple of times. My sister went with me on the first Sunday, which was Mother's Day. The next Sunday I went to just love on the people and let them know I would stay in touch. I had to go into Gary's office and pack his personal belongings and some of his books (leaving many I thought the members could use). Since this was so difficult, a church member went with me and stayed until I was finished, helping me place items in the car. I had to decide that it would always be too painful for me to sit in the small chapel and constantly be reminded of Gary. Members seemed to understand. So, now, where was I to go? My sister invited me to be a part of her church, a different denomination. Again, I did not seem to belong anywhere at all, but I remember Laura saying, "Give it a year and you will feel a part of this church too." She was right. I became part of a Sunday School class, and began reaching out to the home-bound and making new friends. A year after Gary's death, I looked around the church with a happier heart, realizing that so many new friends were now part of my life.

2. Did anyone say anything to you that was especially helpful after his death? Anything that added to your pain?

So many things were said to me that were thoughtful, helpful, comforting. Of course, I knew that some people just want you to "move on," "get on with life." One person actually said to me, "You've been a pastor's wife, so you know what you are supposed to do--pull yourself up by your bootstraps and go on with life!!!"

A few well-meaning friends wanted me to be happy as I always had been, wanted me to be "fine," and really did not want to let me talk about my grief. Some gave me a "time table" for my grief to be over.

However, I was fortunate to receive so many loving messages. Since I did not want to forget them, I typed them into my computer so that I would have them when I needed to be reminded how much people loved Gary and me. It is difficult to pick a few, but maybe these I've chosen will be helpful to someone. I am scrolling through the 54 small print pages I recorded of those messages from dear people.

A long-time friend: "There is no time limit on grief. It takes a very long time. And I KNOW that God is truly never more near. Just as He sent us His Comforter when He Himself arose....the Holy Spirit....so does He send us added, meaningful comfort when our most beloved ones have to leave us. I don't see any conflict in that. During grief, I believe the Lord sends us thoughts, dreams, experiences, moments that get us through and remind us that He is so aware of our pain, that He is with us, and that He cares so much. I think He blesses us very specially at this time. I can almost imagine Gary, just on the other side of Jesus, asking about you.....as much as you think of, wonder, and ask about him."

Many others wrote on Gary's birthday, which was 14 days after his death. One said, "Dear Bertha, I just had to tell you that I am remembering you today on Gary's birthday. It must be such a sad and difficult time for you. I can't make it any easier I know, but I just wanted you to know I care about you so much and am praying for you. I can just imagine how happy you must have made all the birthdays you had together. I do hope that you will find joy in those memories and in the knowledge that today with Jesus surpasses every good thing experienced on earth. May his grace and love cover you today. I love you."

Some practical advice was also given:

"It is always important to have something planned to do when you get up."

"Be careful when you're driving because we don't think straight in our grief."

"At bedtime, say aloud, 'Father, I know I am not alone--You are here with me' ; 'I will lie down in peace and sleep.' Saying it aloud just confirms it."

"It took me a long time before I could realize that I didn't have to get back home."

"Gary did what he came to do, what God planned for him to do; he was faithful to his calling."

"I keep an aluminum baseball bat under my bed" (smiling).

When I told an older Christian man (84 at the time) who had always been a support to our ministry that every time I heard something new I automatically wanted to tell Gary that, he told me, "Don't be afraid to talk to him. My mother died when I was five-years-old. Sometimes, even now I say, 'Momma, I don't know what to do here--will you help me." How very sweet and helpful!

I told my sister and a trusted friend in my raw grief, "I don't even know if I really am trusting God--maybe I've always just been a part of what Gary was doing." My sister said, "Now you will; you will become stronger; you will experience God for yourself." My friend who had lost her husband years ago said in the same visit, "I didn't think I was anything--I had always been my husband's wife--that was my identity. I didn't know what I was, but God has shown me who I am."

A friend told me, "It's been two years since my husband died, and I still have days now and then when I just seem to fall apart. It's okay because it is just now and then."

Another would call me from time to time even though it had been years since Gary was her pastor. She told me, "You never get over grieving, but it does get easier."

A friend I talked with almost daily in the couple of years after Gary's death would gave me "pictures" to think about as she knows I need those. One day I thought I was having a good day, but suddenly felt I was back at the beginning of my grief. She told me, "Picture yourself in this wide, very deep and dark hole. Someone has put a ladder down for you, and you begin slowly and carefully, with much weakness try to ascend the ladder. One day you reach another rung and then another; finally you can begin to see a glimmer of light somewhere piercing the darkness. Suddenly, your foot slips, and you go back a rung or two. That's where your grief is now, but you are not where you started, you are moving forward." I have kept that mental image all of this time.

3. What have you learned about grief as a result of dealing with this? Give as many lessons as you can think of.

* "There is no time limit on grief"; a year (or 13 months, some say) seems to be the "magic" time. For others, it is a lifetime.

*Some people cope better than others, are able to navigate this new life with greater ease. It is all personal; there is no "size fits all."

*Deep and prolonged grief does not necessarily mean the love was greater than that of the person who seems to heal more quickly.

*A tendency to withdraw from others is often a response to a loved one's death. This may be temporary as it was for me, or it may become a pattern for others.

*Anger often enters the picture. Anger can be at God for taking the loved one, but if not at God, it can be anger toward people in general who still have their loved ones. As my sister said to me when I was going through a phase of anger, "Bertha, no one did this to you." That made sense and helped diffuse my anger.

*Those who haven't lost a loved one do not and cannot understand the depth of grief, for they haven't experienced it, and we wouldn't want anyone to have to be more anxious about their own future of loss.

*When people ask, "How are you?" most want you to say, "I'm fine." In my case, I could not say that because I wasn't fine. I learned to say, "I'm okay." I learned I did not have to give any platitudes and say anything I did not mean. There are only a few in our circle of friends who can bear to listen over a period of time (and want to listen) to the great pain that envelops the soul. I am so thankful for some very close friends who encouraged me in that way.

*A friend who lost her husband listened to her relatives say, "Well he is in a better place and not hurting anymore . . ." She replied, "Yes, he is, but I'm still here." We are thankful that our loved one is with the Lord, but we wish either that we were there with him or that the pain of grief would go away.

*There does come a time (different for every person) when the grief is not as raw and painful. For me, it was over a year and a half. I had always felt there was a searing knife cutting into my inner being, but one day while walking my dog, I realized the knife was not there. I said, "Lord, what is happening to me?" I wanted to clutch the knife back, for it was what I had of Gary, and I was afraid of losing that connection, it seemed.

*Having a job to do is important. If a wife loses her husband and she has children to raise, she knows life has to go on for them. I have read that if one already has a job to go to and responsibilities to attend to, it helps with the grief; however, if one goes out to secure a job in order to "get away" from the grief, the grief will be prolonged. Since I teach at a local community college, I had to be in class, teach, grade papers, and relate to students. This was a great help to have something to focus on other than myself.

*Grief Counseling can be helpful to most people as one finds the hard experiences are actually very common and quite normal. Coping mechanisms provided by professionals can be invaluable. Associating with a group enables one to see that others are suffering too.

*Most people cannot put advice into their brains at the time of their grief. Just knowing someone cares, is praying for them, checks on them, includes them in some of their times with other friends, and sometimes cries with them makes a great deal of difference.

4. What advice do you have for people who have lost a spouse or a child in death?

*Do the necessary things: make the bed (this keeps you from crawling back in and sleeping all day); take care of your personal needs (shower; wash and style your hair; put on your make-up; take off your robe and dress for the day--you will feel better about yourself when you look in the mirror); wash the dishes; do the laundry; sweep and vacuum; sort the mail and throw away what isn't needed; pay the bills; wash the car; prepare balanced, regular meals (even if you are not hungry--you need to stay healthy in order to better deal with all the stress); exercise (whatever you have been used to except do not overdo it. If you are not used to doing any exercise, start walking short distances and build up); if you have a job, go back to work after the agreed upon time, and let co-workers befriend you.

*Take time to spend with the Lord (keep a schedule you've already established; if you are used to having time with the Lord in the morning or evening, stay with your comfortable time).

*Let people "in." Accept invitations even when you do not feel like going. If you never accept, soon the invitations will dry up.

*Be good to yourself; do some things you haven't had time to do before.

*Rest when you are weary (physically or emotionally); keep a timer close by so you do not sleep an inordinate amount of time.

*A verse that meant so much to me is Isaiah 61:3, "To all who mourn . . . He will give: Beauty for ashes; Joy instead of mourning; Praise instead of heaviness" (LVB).

*I don't know when your grief will lessen, but if we daily spend time with the Lord, telling him all about our feelings that day (and all during the day), asking Him to direct our every step and the focus of our minds, one day we will be aware that He is, indeed, lessening our pain, and giving us a "window" of hope into our earthly journey.

PART 4

What to Say to a Hurting Friend

People are always wondering, "What is the right thing to say?"

What follows is a piece inspired by (and mostly written) by my Washington State friend Holly Rollosson. When we posted it on our website, it quickly went viral.

"Comfort, O comfort my people, says your God" (Isaiah 40:1).

Recently, while talking to Holly and her mother, I began to pick up on some truly bizarre things people said to them after Holly's young-adult brother Seth's tragic automobile accident that left him severely disabled, completely helpless, and almost totally without the ability to communicate. Holly describes his condition as "a low level of consciousness due to a profound brain injury."

Frankly, I was stunned by some of the things people have said to this family. I had no idea God's people could be so thoughtless, so clueless, so heartless–all in the name of the Lord and ostensibly, with the best of intentions.

After our visit, I asked if they would share with us some of the things people have said over the several years Seth has been in this sad condition.

Holly wants to emphasize that *all the Christian folks who said these things to them have good intentions. Everyone genuinely thinks they're offering something helpful.* Holly is probably more charitable than I. Not everyone who deigns to speak for God has the best interests of others at heart.

Here they are, in the order in which she sent them along, along with my comment underneath....

1. "If you just had enough faith, your son would be healed."

The variations on this theme were endless. One wonders where people came up with the notion that God will heal everyone who has faith enough. Do they think the hospitals are populated only by the sinful and faithless?

2. "God wants to heal your brother. It's your parents' fault that he does not sit up in that bed, completely restored, because they will not get rid of their doubts and have faith!"

Holly said, "The poor guy. Apparently, God really wants to heal Seth, but His hands are tied because the victim's parents don't have enough faith!"

If the Lord healed everyone of everything, no one would ever die. The story of Job clearly speaks to this erroneous idea that suffering is always the result of sin. All we have to do now is get the Lord's people to read the Bible.

3. "You need to have faith, not that your son can be healed, but to believe beyond a shadow of a doubt that he is already healed, and he will be."

Holly says, "Now that one just does not begin to make sense!" I respond, "You haven't been listening to the right faith healers on television, my sister."

The "name it and claim it" philosophy holds that believing it strongly enough makes it a reality. The best answer to this shallow heresy is: "Preach it in Haiti. Let's see those people prosper. Then we will listen to you."

4. "What do you think God is trying to teach you through this?"

This is the fix-it mentality. People see a tragedy and want to make it right. Never mind that they are not capable and are giving counsel far out of their field of expertise, assuming they have one.

5. "Remember, pastor—" (Oh! Did I tell you that Holly and Seth's father is a pastor?) "It says in Romans that 'God works all things together for good.'"

The family wishes they had a nickel for each time they've heard that. Holly comments that it falls under the category of "trite but true."

6. "You know, you're really lucky. I've heard that being an empty-nester is really hard. Now, you'll never have to go through that!"

The reason he will never leave home is that Seth will remain completely dependent on his parents' care the rest of his life. His life-expectancy (I asked about this) is around 15 years, most of which he has already lived in this condition.

7. "You know, you're really lucky. I was watching a TV show last night that said those who use their brains every day are less likely to become senile in old age. So taking care of your son is keeping you young and sharp."

I know, I know. You're doubting that anyone actually said something this inane. They did.

8. "Here's why I think God did this."

The family member on the receiving end of this bit of wisdom thinks to him/herself, "Really? You presume to know the mind of God?"

9. "You must feel glad that where your son is now"–in a semi-vegetative state– "he can no longer sin!"

You know, the ability to sin is not the worst thing in the world. The inability to sin (or anything else!) at all is far, far worse.

10. (In response to Mary's saying she was exhausted from the 24/7 routine of caring for Seth, including rising in the middle of the night, every night, someone said:) "Well, you know, it's not such a big deal. Lots of people who have newborn babies at home have to do the same thing."

There are times when we do well just to keep our mouths shut and say nothing. Sadly, this person missed a great opportunity to be quiet.

11. "I would like to pay to have (a certain faith healer) come and pray over your son. I'm confident that would heal him. In the meantime, here is a stack of that preacher's materials to look over."

At what point does a parent violate their own beliefs and convictions in order to bless their needy child? But welcoming into your home a so-called "faith healer" is something else altogether.

12. "If your son would just stop raging in his heart against God, then God would be free to heal him."

Holly wonders, "How do you know what a guy in a coma is thinking?"

Personally, I would have shown the visitor the door and ordered them off my property. Enough is enough.

13. "I know your brother is going to wake up! People wake up from comas all the time. I saw it on television last week!"

Holly wishes she had a nickel for every time someone has thrown that one their way. She thinks, "Wouldn't it be nice if real life always resolved itself at the end of a 30-minute time slot, just like on television."

14. "We want to be your family . We want to be there for you, every week. Twice a week if you need it."

The people who said that never returned or even inquired as to how Seth and the family were doing.

15. "You know, it's been 7 years. You really need to get over this and move on."

That's pretty hard to do when your loved one is lying in the next room, requiring 24/7 personal care.

16. "I want to come visit your son, but I just can't. You see, I don't do well in hospitals." Or, this

variation: "I just can't handle seeing him like this. I want to remember him the way he was."

What goes through your mind on hearing this is: "Maybe you need to get over yourself, friend. Think of what it must be like to be in his condition. Think how much it might mean to him to hear the voice of a friend."

17. "I know how you feel." "I know what you're going through."

No, you don't. The only person who knows is one who has been there themselves. When our family pastor's teenage son was killed on a motorcycle, the community was devastated. One lady coming through the line told the grieving father, "I know how you feel. When my son went off to college, I thought I would die." The pastor felt like asking, "Is your son coming home? Because my son is never coming home again."

18. "We're on our way home from a workshop on faith healing, and we'd like to stop by and pray over your brother!"

This couple left with a rather disappointed air when the new techniques they had learned failed to work.

19. "The other night we stopped by the hospital after everyone was gone. I prayed healing over your brother, called him forth, and said, 'Young man, arise!'"

They seemed to feel a certain satisfaction over having done this. One wonders why, since Seth continued to lie there.

20. *"I want to come and pray for your son." "I want to come and minister to you."*

They stayed an additional three hours during which time they talked about themselves, their kids' activities, politics, and last Friday night's football game.

Holly observes, "People like this genuinely believe they mean it when they say they want to come pray for you and/or minister to you. But what they really mean is they want to sit and have someone listen to them talk all afternoon."

Such people leave thinking–as a woman said in church one day–"Wow, I really ministered to them today! It must have been such a bright spot in their sad situation, to hear my cheerful, fascinating conversation."

On another occasion, a woman known for staying all day became insulted and then rude when the family declined her offer to visit the hospital in a time of crisis.

Holly notes, "Here is a hint for anyone who is considering visiting a sick friend or one in a crisis: Unless you are specifically asked otherwise, limit your visit to a half hour at the most. They have enough to deal with without having to pretend all afternoon to be interested in what your kids are doing."

Holly says a half-hour. I'd say more like 10 or 15 minutes max. Even if you drove two hours to the hospital, you should not feel a longer visit with the family is called for. This is about them, not you.

21. "I am sending you a hankie that has been prayed over by a (certain South American faith healer), who has been known to raise the dead!"

Another said, "I saw your story on the web site and I am sending you a special 1-inch square of fabric to put under his pillow, which will heal him. I'll get back in touch with you in a couple of weeks to hear about all the improvements."

The gullibility of some people knows no bounds.

NOW, HAVING SAID ALL THAT, HOLLY NOTES THAT MANY PEOPLE WERE WONDERFUL AND SAID THINGS THAT GENUINELY DID BLESS AND ENCOURAGE THEM.

"I'm so sorry." When in doubt, that's the best thing to say.

"Can I pray with you?" Prayer is always welcome.

"Here are some meals to put in your freezer and use when you need them."

Holly suggests, "Rather than asking 'Let me know if there is anything I can do to help'–which will likely be turned down, as no one ever wants to trouble another person–why not say: 'I am going to _____ for you.' Perhaps it's to bring a meal, give you a gas card for all those trips to the hospital, or harvest your garden." She adds, "I've been guilty of it myself. It's a way to sound like you care without really having to do anything, because you know they probably won't take you up on it."

I suspect we're all guilty of this "If there is anything I can do" routine. Holly's parents–and so many in their situation–will almost never call someone and say, "Okay, you said to call you if you could do anything, so we need you."

One young friend took it upon himself *every Sunday* to drive to the care center and sit with Seth until the family arrived from church. He held Seth's hand, prayed aloud for him, and talked with him. Holly says, "We will never forget that kindness."

"I would like to offer to stay with your son for an afternoon so you can get out for a few hours."

Holly notes that Seth's longtime best friend comes by every time he's in town. He helps with projects around the house. Another friend, a firefighter, regularly stops to chat with Seth and exchange theological ideas with Pastor Esvelt. "Both are others-centered," Holly notes, "and are true ministers to us."

88

She adds, "It was amazing how God prompted so many of His people to meet specific needs at just the right time, over and over again."

We will conclude with the single best thing to say in almost all situations—a house fire, a job loss, the death of a friend, whatever. No one has ever improved on this line:

"I'm so sorry." Or, "I love you."

Or both.

Administered with a hug.

You can even add, "My heart is so sad for you."

But then stop.

You said enough. Quit talking, even though the urge is welling up inside you. Squelch it.

You have gotten it perfect.

This Final Word....

Esther, a native of Kenya, lives in the Dallas area now. She shared her story with Joe.

When Esther was in college in her native country, one day a cousin arrived to inform her that her father had died. "There were no cell phones back then," she explained. She had to take the bus home, an arduous ten-hour trip "with a million stops along the way."

When she finally arrived in her hometown, she learned she had missed the funeral. She was beside herself with grief. "I could not get the strength to walk home from the bus stop. My legs literally refused to go to a home where I was an orphan."

"My brothers had to come get me. We cried and we cried." Then, at some point, one of Esther's brothers started singing what she calls "a Catholic song my dad used to sing. We always giggled when he sang it."

Esther's brother sounded so much like their father that the whole family laughed and cried at the same time. "From that, I got the strength to walk home."

She adds, "We still talk about my dad like he is among us. We sing that song, and still laugh like we did then."

Both pain and joy are legitimate. Weeping and rejoicing are valid emotions.

We must not deny either. The Pharisee in us would deny the joy, while weeping is rejected by those who have not come to terms with their humanity.

Scripture calls us to "Rejoice with those who rejoice, and weep with those who weep" (Romans 12:15).

After the incredible insights and revelations concerning our immortality throughout the 15th chapter of I Corinthians, we are given this: "Then shall be brought to pass the saying that is written, 'O death, where is your sting? O grave, where is your victory?'" (15:55)

So, go ahead and laugh at death. Some will think you're into denial and wishing upon a star. But you will know different.

Just on the other side of death a party is going on.

And we've all been invited.

"And the Spirit and the bride say, 'Come.' And let the one who hears say, 'Come.' And let the one who is thirsty come; let the one who wishes take the water of life without cost" (Revelation 22:17).

"Amen. Come, Lord Jesus" (Revelation 22:20).

About the Authors

JOE N. MCKEEVER is a native of Alabama. He has been saved more than 60 years, has been preaching the gospel more than 50 years, and has been writing and cartooning for Christian publications more than 40 years. He holds a bachelor's degree from Birmingham-Southern College and both a masters and doctorate from New Orleans Baptist Theological Seminary. Joe has three children and eight grandchildren. He and his wife Bertha live in a suburb of Jackson, Mississippi.

Follow Joe's writings at www.joemckeever.com.

BERTHA FAGAN MCKEEVER is a native of Mississippi. She graduated from Bob Jones University and holds a masters degree from Rhode Island College. She has two children and six grandchildren. Bertha has taught high school and college English almost all her adult life. She loves to bake banana bread to share with friends far and wide, to crochet afghans for loved ones, and to grow flowers around her house. Bertha is beloved by every student who has ever sat in her classes, and each one is special to her. Of all the roles she has filled throughout her life, being a pastor's wife is her favorite. Her favorite Scripture is Proverbs 3:5-6.

CPSIA information can be obtained
at www.ICGtesting.com
Printed in the USA
BVHW070157221120
593552BV00004B/8